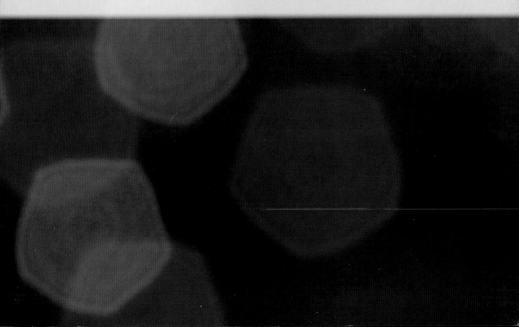

CONTEMPORARY LIVES

JENNIFER LOPEZ

ACTRESS & POP SUPERSTAR

JENNIFER LOPEZ

ACTRESS & POP SUPERSTAR

by Kristine Carlson Asselin

CREDITS

Published by ABDO Publishing Company, PO Box 398166, Minneapolis, MN 55439. Copyright © 2013 by Abdo Consulting Group, Inc. International copyrights reserved in all countries. No part of this book may be reproduced in any form without written permission from the publisher. The Essential Library™ is a trademark and logo of ABDO Publishing Company.

Printed in the United States of America,
North Mankato, Minnesota
102012
012013

♻ THIS BOOK CONTAINS AT LEAST 10% RECYCLED MATERIALS.

Editor: Megan Anderson
Series Designer: Emily Love

Cataloging-in-Publication Data

Asselin, Kristine Carlson.
 Jennifer Lopez: actress & pop superstar / Kristine Carlson Asselin.
   p. cm. -- (Contemporary lives)
Includes bibliographical references and index.
ISBN 978-1-61783-621-3
1. Lopez, Jennifer, 1970- --Juvenile literature. 2. Actors--
United States--Biography--Juvenile literature. 3. Singers--United
States--Biography--Juvenile literature. 3. Hispanic American
actors--Biography--Juvenile literature. 4. Hispanic American singers--
Biography--Juvenile literature. 1. Title.
791.4302/8092--dc15
[B]
                                                    2012945989

TABLE OF CONTENTS

When portraying Selena, Lopez lip-synched in front of crowds of the singer's fans.

CHAPTER 1

On the Brink of Stardom

||||||||||||||||||||||||||||||||||||||||||||||||||||||||||||||||||||||||||

Twenty-seven-year-old Jennifer Lopez stood backstage at an arena in San Antonio, Texas, dressed in a purple beaded bodysuit. It was 1996, and the cameras were about to start rolling to capture the opening scene of *Selena*, Lopez's first leading movie role. The concert scene was inspired by Selena Quintanilla Pérez's last real concert at the Houston Astrodome in 1995. Staring out at more than 30,000 people, Lopez said to her mother, Lupe, who had flown in for the occasion, "These are all Selena's fans. What if they start booing?"[1]

> **"It's the most difficult role I've had, because Selena isn't a fictional character—and her family is sitting right in front of me while I'm acting."[4]**
>
> —JENNIFER LOPEZ

Lopez had good reason to be worried. Even though she had spent countless hours practicing the mannerisms and vocal style of murdered Tejano singer Selena and studying tapes of her performances, some members of the Latin community had complained Lopez was the "wrong kind of Latina."[2] Director Gregory Nava had selected Lopez, a New York City native born to Puerto Rican parents, to play the role of the Mexican-American singer. Nava said, "It was a little hurtful. [The protesters] should be celebrating that we have an all-Latino cast and that Jennifer Lopez, one of our own, is becoming a star."[3]

Tejano is the Spanish word for "Texan" and describes Texans of Mexican heritage. The term is also often used to describe language, art, music, and food. Tejano music can trace its roots to the musical influences of German, Polish, and Czech immigrants who migrated from Europe to Mexico and Texas.

CONTROVERSIAL AUDITION

When Nava was looking for the actress to star in his biopic about Selena, he needed to find someone with a perfect blend of the singer's talent and personality. Staging auditions in multiple cities, the filmmaker saw 22,000 hopefuls who wanted the role. Nava had directed Lopez in 1995's *My Family*. He encouraged her to audition for the title role in *Selena*, telling her, "I can't offer you this role, you have to win it."[5] In the end, Nava thought it was Lopez who captured Selena's energy and talent.

For Lopez, one of the role's biggest challenges was the dancing, even though she was an experienced dancer. "It's very hard to unlearn everything your body is accustomed to doing and that it does naturally," Lopez said. "I had to learn what Selena did, which is very different from my own dance instincts."[6]

Other controversies had surrounded the filming, including fan outrage that Lopez couldn't speak fluent Spanish, even though Selena couldn't either. But Lopez prepared for the role the same way she had for every other character she had played—by doing as much research as possible. She studied interviews, concert performances, and talked with Selena's family members. She hoped all her efforts would make her interpretation of Selena as real and relatable as possible.

Lopez was not new to the acting world. Her parents had encouraged her and her two sisters, Lynda and Leslie, to perform since they were children. She had been taking singing and dancing lessons since she was five. By 1996, she had already appeared on television and in supporting film roles opposite Robin Williams and Jack Nicholson. But playing a beloved star, whose death still resonated among fans, was different. It was the biggest thing Lopez had done up to that point in her career.

As she walked out onto the stage, the huge crowd screamed and cheered. Lopez remembers, "I was dressed like Selena. I looked like Selena. That was one thing we all noticed: they were screaming 'Jennifer' too."[7] As she lip-synched to actual recordings of Selena's songs, Lopez felt the love and support radiating from the crowd. She knew the

SELENA QUINTANILLA PÉREZ

Selena Quintanilla Pérez, known as the "Queen of Tejano Music," was a rising pop sensation in 1995, before her premature death at the age of 23. Selena was born on April 16, 1971, and starting at age nine, she performed with her brother and sister as part of a family act, Selena y Los Dinos. Eventually, Selena signed with the EMI Latin record label and attracted the attention of both the Spanish- and English-speaking communities in the United States and Mexico. Selena was the number one female Latino star in the United States and Mexico before her death.

In March 1995, before Selena could fully realize her potential, Yolanda Saldívar, president of her fan club, brutally murdered her in a hotel room in Corpus Christi, Texas. Saldívar was sentenced to life in prison with no possibility of parole for 30 years. Immediately after her death, Selena became the first artist with five Spanish-language albums on the *Billboard* 200 chart at the same time.

Director Nava was pleased with his selection of Lopez in *Selena*.

hard work she had put into preparing for the role had been worth it.

REACTION TO *SELENA*

Selena opened in March 1997, debuting in second at the box office and grossing almost $12 million during its opening weekend. Selena fans were not the only ones who loved Lopez's portrayal of the singer. Nava had never doubted his decision to hire Lopez for the role, saying,

In January 1998, Lopez received a Golden Globe nomination for Best Performance by an Actress in a Motion Picture—Comedy or Musical for her role in *Selena*. The award ultimately went to actress Helen Hunt, who won for her role in the film *As Good as It Gets*.

There was no question in the world, but that Jennifer Lopez was heads above everybody else. She was stunning. She won that role with her talent.[8]

Critics agreed with Nava about Lopez's performance. Roger Ebert, a veteran film critic for the *Chicago Sun-Times*, called her performance "star-making."[9]

Lopez loved singing and dancing in the opening sequence of the movie at the Astrodome. Listening to people sing along and call out her name was an emotional and powerful moment. That was when Lopez had a life-changing epiphany. After filming the emotional scene, she said to Nava, "I want to do this. I want to be a musical performer."[10] The spark inside her had ignited. Lopez decided to pursue a music career.

||||||||||

Growing up in the Bronx, Jennifer developed a love for dancing.

CHAPTER 2

Early Years

||||||||||||||||||||||||||||||||||||||||||||||||||||||||||||||||||||||||||||||||||

Jennifer Lynn Lopez was born in the Castle Hill neighborhood of the Bronx, New York, on July 24, 1969. Her parents, Guadalupe and David, were both born in Puerto Rico but did not meet until they came to the United States. She is the second of three girls—her sister Leslie is one year older, and Lynda is two years younger.

Jennifer's childhood during the early 1970s was "no different than anybody else" growing up in a Puerto

Rican family in the Bronx.[1] The Lopez girls spent a lot of time with family, playing in the street with neighborhood kids, listening to music, and enjoying good food.

David worked hard at his job as a computer technician to support his family. Guadalupe, known as Lupe, spent her time shuttling the girls to dance classes and encouraging them to sing, dance, and perform in plays. She cheered them on by saying, "God gave you all these talents, you have to go out and do the best that you can."[2]

Even though she encouraged all three girls to do their best, Lupe also criticized the girls and pressed each of them toward one talent. For example, Lupe decided Jennifer was the athletic dancer and often spoke critically of her singing

LYNDA LOPEZ

Lopez's younger sister, Lynda, is an Emmy Award–winning journalist. She has been a news anchor for three television stations in New York. She was also an entertainment reporter on *E! News Live* and contributed to *Latina* magazine's "Making Us Proud" column. Lynda started her career as a radio personality and made her first television appearance as a video jockey (VJ) on the VH1 network.

Godspell is one of the biggest musical theater successes of all time. John-Michael Tebelak wrote the script for the musical, with Stephen Schwartz writing the musical score and lyrics. Based on the Bible's Gospel of Matthew, it tells the story of the final days of Jesus and his disciples from the Last Supper to the Crucifixion. *Godspell* ran off-Broadway from 1971 to 1976 before making its Broadway debut on June 22, 1976. The movie version was filmed in New York City and released in 1973. "Day by Day," the show's biggest song, was an international hit, reaching Number 13 on the *Billboard* chart in July 1972.

because Leslie was supposedly the singer in the family.

Despite her mother's criticism, Jennifer loved and continued all different types of performing. She was a dancer in musicals at the all-girl Catholic Preston High School. Eventually, the dedication paid off. As a junior, Jennifer won a lead role in the musical *Godspell*. Partly due to her mother's lack of confidence in her, she was terrified at the prospect of singing the show's biggest song, "Day by Day." Overwhelmed by stage fright on opening night, her voice wavered as she started the song's first notes. But she pushed through the fear.

With her voice shaking the whole time, she gave the performance everything she had and made it through the choreographed dance routine. To this day, Jennifer considers it a transforming moment in her life that meant "breaking outside of my box . . . breaking outside of what people think I can do."[3]

LIVING THE DREAM

Even though they supported her artistic endeavors for the most part, Lopez's parents always assumed she would continue her education after high school. They wanted her to attend Baruch College in Manhattan and study business. Even though Lopez attended the college for her first semester, she continued to dream about going into show business. But her parents did not want the life of an entertainer for her. The disagreement that followed escalated into a fight that ended with Lupe saying, "If you don't want to live by my rules, there's the door."[4]

In 1986, at 17, Lopez left home to live her dream. Eventually, she found herself living at her dance studio, obsessed with dance classes and

After high school, Lopez decided to pursue her dream of becoming a performer.

trying to make a living as a performer. Lopez had a small role in her first movie, the 1986 low-budget film *My Little Girl*. Unfortunately for Lopez, the life of a glamorous celebrity was still a decade away. She worked as a backup dancer in music videos and live shows, performing with hip-hop recording artists such as MC Hammer and EPMD. The pay was terrible, sometimes only $50 per video for a few days of work. She was barely making enough money to eat—she got by living on cheap pizzas and trying to stretch the cash until the next job came along.

|||||||||||||||||||||||||||||||||||||||||||||||||||

THE BIG BREAK

In November 1990, Lopez heard about auditions for an open spot as a dancer on the sketch comedy show *In Living Color*, which had debuted on the Fox television network in April 1990. Along with what must have seemed like every other dancer in New York City, Lopez waited in a line that stretched around the block to try out for a spot as one of the show's "Fly Girls." Comedian

IN LIVING COLOR |||||||||||||||||||||||||||||||||||||||||||||||||||||||||||||||||||

Brothers Keenen Ivory and Damon Wayans created the groundbreaking sketch comedy show *In Living Color* in 1990. It followed a similar structure as other sketch comedy shows, such as *Saturday Night Live*, but broke new ground with its smart—often borderline offensive—content. Specifically targeting African-American audiences, the Wayans spoofed and poked fun at cultural references most people would not have touched for fear of offending. *In Living Color* helped launch the careers of actors Jamie Foxx, Jim Carrey, and David Alan Grier. It also helped the careers of its creators, the Wayans, and their siblings, Kim, Shawn, Marlon, and Dwayne.

Keenen Ivory Wayans, the show's creator and host, remembered Lopez's audition:

> I had been there six hours and seen every dancer in New York and I was almost ready to give up and then this young girl steps up and the spotlight landed on her and she captivated everyone in the room.[5]

On September 22, 1991, at the age of 22, Lopez landed a role as a Fly Girl on *In Living Color*. For two seasons, Lopez performed on the show under the tutelage of actor and dancer Rosie Perez, the choreographer for *In Living Color*.

In 1993, Lopez made the decision to leave the show to pursue her acting career. She landed small roles in TV series and made-for-TV movies. In 1994, Lopez won a small role in *My Family*, a movie cowritten and directed by Gregory Nava. Both *My Family* and *Money Train*, Lopez's first action-comedy film, premiered in 1995. *Money Train* costarred popular actors Woody Harrelson and Wesley Snipes.

In late 1995, Lopez went to Miami, Florida, to start filming her next role as Gabriela in the film *Blood and Wine*. The film starred veteran actor

Lopez had a small role as Young Maria in *My Family.*

Jack Nicholson, as well as Stephen Dorff. While in Miami, Lopez met waiter Ojani Noa, and the two began dating.

In 1996, Lopez appeared opposite Robin Williams in *Jack*, a film by legendary film director Francis Ford Coppola about a boy with a rare aging disorder. Lopez's role of Miss Marquez was originally written as an older white woman, but Lopez made it her own. Most of Lopez's roles had been small and supporting, but she was getting good reviews from critics and fans.

SELENA

In 1996, Nava staged a national casting call for his new movie about slain singing sensation Selena Quintanilla Pérez. He scheduled auditions in San Antonio, Texas; Los Angeles, California; Chicago, Illinois; and Miami, Florida. In San Antonio alone, more than 6,000 hopefuls lined up for the opportunity to audition. Nava had worked with Lopez on *My Family* and asked her to audition for the part.

Lopez's audition included acting out a few scenes from the movie and performing two of Selena's songs. Of the audition, Lopez said, "There's no way you can put a character together for an audition, but you can give the idea of whether you have the required charisma and the ability to do it."[6] When she was selected for the role, it ignited controversy that the open casting call had been a publicity stunt. But Nava was certain Lopez was the right actor for the role, saying, "The combination of her enormous talent, warmth, appeal, and strength made her the ideal candidate to portray Selena."[7] Lopez was about to star in the role of a lifetime.

||||||||||

Lopez and Noa married on
February 22, 1997.

CHAPTER 3

Making Music

||||||||||||||||||||||||||||||||||||||||||||||||||||||||||||||||||||||||||||||||||||

After winning the role of Selena, Lopez threw herself into rehearsals and research for the role.

The time and energy Lopez spent studying the talented and hardworking Selena left her with a burning desire to make her own music. Performing the musical numbers "was really the impetus and really kind of like the spark inside of me. I was just like, this is what I always wanted to do," Lopez said.[1]

> "All I could think about was I have to be so good in this; I need to watch everything of [Selena's] that ever existed. I need to hear every song she ever made. I need to talk to everybody in her life."[2]
>
> —*JENNIFER LOPEZ*

Lopez also left the set of *Selena* with a huge diamond engagement ring from boyfriend Ojani Noa. Lopez had fallen in love with the waiter and aspiring model, who proposed in front of the entire *Selena* cast at the film's wrap party. They married on February 22, 1997, despite her mother's concerns that Noa was using Lopez for her money.

In March 1997, *Selena* was released in theaters. For the first time, Lopez found real fame thrust upon her as critics raved about her performance. Suddenly, strangers in the street knew Lopez by name, and she began suffering anxiety attacks. Sadly, her relationship with Noa was one of the first casualties of her fame. After only 11 months, Lopez and Noa split in January 1998. It would be the first of several romantic heartbreaks.

Just a few weeks after *Selena* opened, Lopez's second action-adventure film came out on

> **"Selena was a spirit. Nothing was going to stop her. And I admire that kind of drive."[4]**
>
> —*JENNIFER LOPEZ*

April 11. In *Anaconda*, Lopez starred opposite veteran actor Jon Voight.

Lopez's character, Terri Flores, had some close calls with a snake in *Anaconda*, which gave Lopez the opportunity to perform her own stunts. "If I can, if it's not too dangerous, I'll do it," Lopez said. "For me, the action stuff in this kind of movie is fun."[3] *Anaconda* didn't have the same critical acclaim as *Selena*, but *Anaconda* did well at the box office that summer. It opened in first place at the box office and took in more than $65 million domestically.

The crime-thriller *U Turn,* Lopez's third film released in 1997, came out in October. It was directed by Oliver Stone and boasted an all-star cast including actors Sean Penn and Nick Nolte. *U Turn*, however, earned less than $7 million domestically before closing.

CROSSING OVER

Even as she landed more movie roles, Lopez still felt the spark to make music, which drove her to change career directions. Lopez had always loved singing, so for her, it was nothing new. Unfortunately, the people around Lopez weren't convinced. Her managers tried to talk her out of the idea, certain it would be a disaster for her blossoming acting career.

But Lopez decided to go with her heart. She fired her managers and used her own money to record a demo album in Spanish. The demo caught the attention of the chairman and chief executive officer (CEO) of Sony Music Entertainment,

TOMMY MOTTOLA

Mottola was born July 14, 1949, in the Bronx, New York. He is a music industry mogul responsible for discovering talents such as singing group Hall and Oates and singer Mariah Carey, as well as Lopez. He has worked with singers John Mellencamp, Carly Simon, and Jessica Simpson, and the female country group the Dixie Chicks. Mottola famously married Carey in 1993, but they divorced in 1997. Mottola later married Mexican pop star Thalía in 2000.

Tommy Mottola. Mottola signed Lopez to record an album for Sony's Epic Records.

> **"Jennifer has tremendous attitude—and I say that in a positive way—and it comes across onscreen and in person, and she puts that into her singing."[7]**
>
> *—TOMMY MOTTOLA*

Lopez was thrilled about signing with Mottola and the record label. But her lack of confidence about being a singer, which stemmed from her childhood, rushed back in full force while making the album. Particularly, while recording "Theme from Mahogany (Do You Know Where You're Going To)," a song originally recorded by legendary singer Diana Ross. Lopez said, "I can't match Diana Ross!"[5] Cory Rooney, the album's executive producer, told her, "Don't worry about Diana Ross, worry about Jennifer. Express this song the way it feels and means to you."[6] Lopez listened to Rooney and put her heart and soul into the album.

ON THE 6

While recording her album, *On the 6*, Lopez listened to other music for inspiration. She became a huge fan of Latin singer Marc Anthony. Coincidentally, they were both recording in the same building, and the two formed a friendship. Lopez's album contained two Spanish-language songs, including a duet with Anthony, the song "No Me Ames." They dated very briefly, but the relationship didn't work out.

Soon after, Lopez met a young hip-hop artist and entrepreneur named Sean "P. Diddy" Combs. Combs was a charismatic entertainer, as well as the owner of a clothing line, restaurants, and the head of his own record label, Bad Boy Records. Combs asked Lopez to appear in his music video for "Been Around the World," which features rappers Notorious B.I.G. and Mase.

It did not take long for Combs to fall in love with Lopez, and soon the two were inseparable. Combs introduced Lopez to Benny Medina, whom she hired as her new manager. Medina embraced all of her talents and set out to help

Lopez met Combs while recording her first album, *On the 6*.

Lopez take full advantage of her singing and acting abilities.

On the 6 was released on June 1, 1999. The album's title referenced the train Lopez rode when she was growing up. Lopez hoped the album would appeal to people who shared her background.

When Lopez heard her first single on the radio, "If You Had My Love," she could hardly believe it. She said, "It's just the craziest feeling

BENNY MEDINA

Benny Medina was born January 24, 1958, in Los Angeles, California. When he was eight, his mother died and his father abandoned him. Medina and his four siblings lived on the streets before moving in with their aunt. By the time he was 12, Medina was back on the streets to escape his aunt's abusive husband.

At a community center, Medina befriended Allen Elliott, the son of a successful television and film composer. The Elliotts allowed Medina to live in their Beverly Hills garage. He made important connections at Beverly Hills High School, including Kerry Gordy, the son of Motown Records founder Berry Gordy. As a high school senior, Medina signed a recording contract with Motown and ended up as an executive working for Gordy. In 1990, Medina's story inspired the NBC series *The Fresh Prince of Bel-Air*, featuring rapper-actor Will Smith.

"If You Had My Love" was Lopez's first single released from *On The 6*. It was cowritten by one of the album's producers, Rodney Jerkins, a songwriter and musician who has worked with popular artists such as Whitney Houston and Michael Jackson. "If You Had My Love" hit Number 1 on the *Billboard* charts on June 12, 1999. The song's music video, directed by Paul Hunter, was particularly popular.

It won the 1999 *Billboard* Music Video Award for Best Pop Video Clip. It was also nominated for four MTV Video Music Awards (VMAs), including Best Female Video, Best Dance Video, Best Pop Video, and Best New Artist. Ten years after it was released, the music video was uploaded to the video-sharing Web site YouTube, and as of June 2012 it had more than 24 million views.

in the world to hear your voice coming through the radio."[8] Released in May 1999, it shot to Number 1 on the *Billboard* chart by early June 1999. With the success of her debut album, Lopez's star was starting to rise very fast.

||||||||||

By 1999, Lopez had successfully crossed over from actress to pop star.

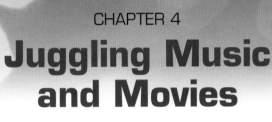

CHAPTER 4

Juggling Music
and Movies

||||||||||||||||||||||||||||||||||||||||||||||||||||||||||||||||||||||

Lopez's debut album, *On the 6,* had generated four top ten hits and sold more than 7 million copies worldwide. After reaching success with *On the 6* in 1999, Lopez knew she had made the right decision about starting a music career.

But she had not given up making movies. She starred in two films released in 1998. The first was *Out of Sight,* a

"Waiting for Tonight," Lopez's second single from *On the 6*, was released in November 1999. It debuted at Number 8 on the *Billboard* Hot 100 on December 4, 1999, and remained on the Hot 100 for 20 weeks. Lopez performed the song live when she opened the *Billboard* Music Awards on December 8, 1999. "Waiting for Tonight" also won the MTV VMA for Best Dance Video in September 2000. *On the 6* also contains a Spanish version of the song, "Una Noche Más."

critically acclaimed action movie costarring actor George Clooney. Lopez portrayed a US marshal who has an affair with a bank robber, played by Clooney.

Out of Sight, from acclaimed director Steven Soderbergh, received nominations for two Academy Awards, Best Film Editing and Best Adapted Screenplay. Lopez won an ALMA Award for Outstanding Actress in a Feature Film in a Crossover Role for *Out of Sight,* as well as nominations for the MTV Movie Awards for Best Female Performance and Best Kiss. In 2011, *Entertainment Weekly* placed *Out of Sight* at the top of its 25 Sexiest Movies list, due to the on-screen chemistry between Lopez and Clooney.

Critics recognized Lopez and Clooney's chemistry in *Out of Sight*.

In September 1998, Lopez starred in her first voice-acting role as Azteca in the animated film *Antz*. *Antz*, the second fully computer-animated feature film following 1995's *Toy Story*, also features the talents of actors Sylvester Stallone,

Woody Allen, and Sharon Stone. Acclaimed by critics, *Antz* earned a number of accolades as well as more than $90 million at the box office.

|||||||||||||||||||||||||||||||||||||||||||||||||||||||||||||||||||||

MAKING HEADLINES

Lopez's personal life seemed to be on the right track as well. Lopez and Combs had a similar work ethic, they came from similar backgrounds, and Combs mentored her in the music industry. Their romance heated up very quickly, and they seemed to be living the typical Hollywood lifestyle. The paparazzi took notice of the pair, and they made headlines wherever they went.

But on December 27, 1999, Lopez and Combs went to a nightclub in New York City, along with a few of Combs's friends. Although they had planned a night of hanging out and dancing, the night ended with a disagreement in the club's private party room. Gunshots were fired, injuring three people. Lopez, Combs, and their entourage quickly left the club after the chaos erupted. Lopez and Combs were arrested after police found a loaded pistol in the car they used to leave the scene.

Lopez called on manager Medina's help following a controversial nightclub shooting in December 1999.

Handcuffed to a pole at the police station, sitting on a bench, Lopez experienced one of the worst nights of her life. Lopez called her manager, Medina, in the middle of the night and begged him to come to the station and get them out of jail. By the end of the night, Lopez was ultimately cleared of any wrongdoing and released from jail. Combs, however, was charged with four counts of illegal possession of a gun and one count of bribery.

|||||||||||||||||||||||||||||||||||||||||||||||||||||||||||

GRAMMY DRESS

The media frenzy surrounding Lopez grew even stronger at the 2000 Grammy Awards on

VERSACE

Designer Donatella Versace created the infamous green dress Lopez wore to the 2000 Grammy Awards. Versace was born on May 2, 1955, in Reggio di Calabria, Italy. Her brother, Gianni, founded the famous Versace clothing line in the late 1970s. Gianni is often recognized as the first designer to embrace contemporary pop culture in fashion. Some of his famous friends included singers Elton John and Madonna. Originally, Donatella worked in the company's public relations department, but Gianni found her more valuable as his partner and "muse."[1]

Donatella and the rest of the fashion industry were rocked with grief when a serial killer shot and killed Gianni in 1997 outside his mansion in Miami, Florida. After, Donatella took over creative control of the company. Donatella credits the media attention on Lopez's dress as a turning point in her career that helped put Versace back on top of the fashion industry.

February 23. Lopez was nominated for Best Dance Recording for her second *On the 6* single, "Waiting for Tonight." Lopez wore a green silk chiffon dress created by designer Donatella Versace. The dress's neckline plunged to her belly button as Lopez walked the red carpet escorted by Combs. At the ceremony, Lopez ended up losing in her category to singer Cher, who won for her song "Believe."

Lopez loved her Grammy dress and did not think about how the media or the public would receive the provocative, skin-revealing style. But the next day, Lopez realized it was a big deal when her picture appeared on the cover of *USA Today*, accompanied by the headline "Skin is In." One reason Lopez had chosen to wear the dress was because she felt comfortable with her body. Even though her curves sometimes seem to define her

"Even to this day, women thank me for the whole idea of a healthy body image, that you could be voluptuous and it's a beautiful thing."[2]

—JENNIFER LOPEZ

image, Lopez has said she loves being a role model for a healthy body type.

In August 2000, Lopez portrayed social worker Catherine Deane in *The Cell*, directed by Tarsem Singh and costarring with Vince Vaughn and Vincent D'Onofrio. Deane is persuaded by an FBI agent, played by Vaughn, to conduct an experimental virtual therapy and go inside the mind of a serial killer, played by D'Onofrio. To prepare for the role, Lopez went to see a therapist, which she said she found helpful both personally and professionally. And the research paid off: Lopez won the 2001 Blockbuster Entertainment Award for Favorite Actress—Science Fiction.

Even though Combs and Lopez loved each other, when it came to relationships, Lopez considered herself pretty traditional. She valued monogamy, but unfortunately, Combs did not. When Lopez realized they did not share the same values, she made the decision to end the relationship. Just after the breakup, Lopez still supported Combs as he stood trial for the charges stemming from the nightclub incident. On March 16, 2001, Combs was acquitted of all charges. Of ending the romance, Lopez said,

Lopez entered the mind of a serial killer in *The Cell*, directed by Tarsem Singh, *left*.

I wasn't really thinking about what people thought. Or this was good or this was not good for my career . . . I was always this person who operated from her heart, for better or for worse.[3]

||||||||||

Lopez became a romantic leading lady with *The Wedding Planner*.

CHAPTER 5

J.Lo on Top

||||||||||||||||||||||||||||||||||||||||||||||||||||||||||||||

While her romance with Combs fizzled out, Lopez continued working on her second album, *J.Lo*. In January 2001, *J.Lo* debuted at Number 1 on the *Billboard* 200. The album's first single was "Love Don't Cost a Thing," which references Lopez's relationship with Combs, who had a habit of buying her expensive presents. Of the parallel, Lopez said,

That's where I was. I was realizing that more than ever. It's not about cars and jewelry and clothes and all that. That's really nice, but that's not the answer to any problem. Not the answer to your happiness. Not the answer to what's gonna fill you up.[1]

As she promoted her new album, Lopez's new romantic comedy, *The Wedding Planner*, costarring actor Matthew McConaughey, debuted in the top spot at the box office on January 26, 2001. The film eventually grossed more than $94 million worldwide. *Us Weekly* rated it as one of the most romantic movies of all time in 2012. During filming, Lopez had concerns about a pivotal scene in *The Wedding Planner*, in which she danced the tango with McConaughey in a park. Pulling off a difficult dance such as the tango along with "all of the emotional beats of the scene, made it difficult," Lopez said.[2]

With the release of *The Wedding Planner* and her album *J.Lo*, Lopez became the first person in history to have both the top movie and album Number 1 simultaneously. Lopez could not believe the historic statistic, joking, "Are you sure Barbara Streisand didn't do it?"[3]

Lopez married Judd after a monthlong engagement.

In January 2001, Lopez met a new guy, Cris Judd, who was a dancer in the music video for "Love Don't Cost a Thing." The two met while filming the music video in Florida. The complete opposite of the high-profile superstar Combs, Lopez called Judd her "peace," saying, "He just brings me stability in a way that I really needed it."[4] The two announced their engagement in August 2001, and married on September 29, 2001.

Cristan Leenon Judd was born on August 15, 1969, in Abilene, Texas, to a Portuguese father and Filipino mother. He spent much of his childhood in Angeles City in the Philippines. In 1995, Judd got his first big break as a backup dancer for singer Michael Jackson's performance at the MTV VMAs. Judd was later promoted to lead dancer for Jackson's HIStory tour.

In 2003, Judd appeared on the ABC reality show *I'm a Celebrity—Get Me Out of Here!* In 2006, he hosted the WE reality series *Dirty Dancing*. Judd has also appeared in numerous acting roles, as well as serving as choreographer for celebrities such as Steve Martin and Nicole Kidman. Judd remarried in 2009.

Her mother, Lupe, called the marriage a mistake, saying, "One thing about Jen is that she jumps too quickly into relationships."[5]

||||||||||||||||||||||||||||||||||||||||||||||||||||||||||||

BRANCHING OUT

At the same time, Lopez had begun turning her love of fashion into part of her empire. In 2001, she announced the J.Lo by Jennifer Lopez clothing line that included sportswear, swimwear, and a fragrance. The fashion line included a junior

Lopez's style has often been spotlighted at award shows and events.

division and was co-run by Andy Hilfiger, brother of fashion designer Tommy Hilfiger.

Adding a clothing line to her résumé seemed like a natural step for Lopez, who had always been a fashion lover. Launching a clothing line allowed Lopez to share that passion for fashion with the world. "I've always loved the glamour," she said. "I can't shy away from that. I've always been very girly."[6]

> "Jen came out of nowhere and showed people that a movie star could be this really hot rock star as well."[7]
>
> —LYNDA LOPEZ

Shortly after her quick engagement and marriage to Judd, Lopez began shooting her new film, *Gigli,* in December 2001. The film costarred actor Ben Affleck and Lopez spoke highly of her costar. Their chemistry on the set was obvious to everyone, including Lopez's mother, Lupe. "The first day I met Ben and I saw him looking at her, like he didn't know I was there," Lupe said. "And

Lopez has had several nicknames throughout her career: J.Lo, La Lopez, and Jenny from the Block. Jenny from the Block comes from one of Lopez's singles, where she sings, "Don't be fooled by the rocks that I got/ I'm still, I'm still Jenny from the block."[10] Lopez was first called J.Lo while dating Combs, and it is a name that has stuck with her ever since. Lopez's friends call her the Supernova.

I sensed there was something there from the first moment I met him."[8]

Once filming on *Gigli* wrapped, Lopez also premiered her latest thriller, *Enough*. The film opened on May 24, 2002, and tells the story of Slim, a woman who fights to save herself and her daughter from her abusive husband. Lopez said of the movie,

> *It's about empowering yourself in any situation. . . . When I read the script, I saw it as, you have the power within yourself, no matter how severe the situation can be, to change whatever that is, to find that power within yourself to change any negative situation.*[9]

||||||||||

Lopez and Affleck were the center of media attention throughout their relationship.

CHAPTER 6

Building a Brand

||||||||||||||||||||||||||||||||||

Unfortunately, as her mother predicted, Lopez's marriage to Judd did not last long. Nine months after the wedding, the marriage ended in divorce in June 2002. Some reports speculated Lopez did not like Judd's frequent nights out partying. Others speculated Judd's motivation behind the split was Lopez's attraction to Affleck.

But Lopez attributed the split to their lives going in different directions. Ultimately, similar to most of her breakups, the divorce was amicable, and the two were able to stay friendly. Lopez later said of Judd, "He's a wonderful person. And it was a tough thing for me in the sense that I never wanted to hurt anybody . . ."[1] Lopez even acknowledged her impulsive nature and her tendency to not always consider the future. "I'm a very 'in the moment' person," Lopez said.[2]

The *Gigli* set reports about Lopez and Affleck also appeared to be true. The two started publically dating after her divorce from Judd was final. "I kind of felt like maybe he might be my Prince Charming, but I'd thought that twice before," Lopez said of Affleck.[3]

||||||||||||||||||||||||||||||||||||||||||||||||||||||||

SMELLING SUCCESS

While sorting out her personal relationships, Lopez had also been developing her first fragrance. She worked in collaboration with Coty, a French company famous for its beauty products and fragrances. Glow by JLo was introduced in September 2002. The perfume targeted a young

Benjamin Geza Affleck-Boldt was born in Berkeley, California, on August 15, 1972, but his family moved to Cambridge, Massachusetts, shortly after his birth. There, he met lifelong friend and fellow actor Matt Damon. After moving to Los Angeles, Affleck had a few minor successes in 1993's *Dazed and Confused* and 1995's *Mallrats*. But his breakout success came when he reunited with friend Damon to cowrite the screenplay for *Good Will Hunting*. The 1997 film grossed more than $130 million and starred Affleck, Damon, and actor Robin Williams. Affleck and Damon won the 1998 Academy Award for Best Original Screenplay. He married actress Jennifer Garner in 2005. In 2007, Affleck made his directorial debut with *Gone Baby Gone*, which starred his younger brother, Casey.

female demographic, which made up Lopez's primary fan base. Lopez partnered with Macy's department store, and in its first year, Glow brought in more than $100 million in sales.

Lopez also returned to the studio in 2002 to work on her third album, *This is Me . . . Then.* Her relationship with Affleck inspired much of Lopez's songwriting on the new album. She even titled one of the love songs "Dear Ben." Affleck and Lopez became engaged in November 2002. Lopez said,

In May 2012, Lopez celebrated the tenth anniversary of her first perfume, Glow. Since its release, the perfume has made more than $1 billion in sales for Coty, which produces the fragrance. With the launch of Glow, Lopez was credited with reviving celebrity fragrance lines, which had mostly died out in the 1980s.

"The whole album, with the exception of one or two songs, was about that time in my life, which had a lot to do with him."[4]

This is Me . . . Then was released on November 26, 2002. The album also created a new nickname for Lopez with its first single, "Jenny from the Block." The song assures fans Lopez is still the same girl from the old neighborhood in the Bronx, despite her fame and fortune.

Lopez ended a busy year with the release of another romantic comedy, *Maid in Manhattan*, on December 13, 2002. The film costarred actor Ralph Fiennes as a politician who falls for a hotel maid whom he mistakes for a wealthy socialite. The romantic comedy genre was proving to be a good

Maid in Manhattan was another successful romantic comedy for Lopez.

fit for Lopez. *Maid in Manhattan* grossed more than $93 million in the United States.

TABLOID PRESSURE

By 2003, the superstar couple nicknamed "Bennifer" had become the center of media attention. By this point in her career, Lopez was used to being the fodder for tabloids and the paparazzi. For her, the constant attention surrounding her daily life was nothing new. Lopez did not think twice about going out in public with Affleck or whether they would be followed. Of the constant attention on their relationship, Lopez said, "I think we were on the cover of magazines every week for almost two years straight."[5]

But the press had never hounded Affleck in the same way before, and he had difficulty handling the constant scrutiny of their private moments. In August 2003, *Gigli* opened to mostly negative reviews. In the theaters for only three weeks, the movie grossed just more than $6 million.

BENNIFER

The tabloids coined the nickname "Bennifer" to refer to Lopez and Affleck while they were dating. This started a popular trend of nicknaming celebrity couples. Actors Brad Pitt and Angelina Jolie have been referred to as "Brangelina," while now-divorced Tom Cruise and Katie Holmes were called "TomKat."

Jessica Blatt, entertainment editor for *CosmoGirl* magazine, says of the trend: "In a celebrity-crazed culture, it's just yet another way for people to put labels in their head and create a hierarchy. It's like in high school we all had names for the 'it' couple, even [if] it was just calling them the 'it' couple."[6]

But the media pressure eventually took its toll on their relationship. Lopez and Affleck ended up cancelling their wedding just a few days before the big day in September 2003. Lopez took the bad press about *Gigli* and their relationship in stride. "I wasn't one that really cared about that kind of thing, but some people do," Lopez later said of the media scrutiny. "Some people can't handle that type of scrutiny or judgment. I think [Affleck] had a hard time with it."[7]

MANAGEMENT CHANGES

Lopez also dealt with another breakup in 2003. She ended her relationship with Medina, her manager of five years. Medina had been instrumental in Lopez's rise to fame and also rumored to be partly responsible for creating her reputation as a demanding diva. Medina made excessive and expensive demands on behalf of his client, such as private planes and over-the-top dressing rooms. "I had such a reputation, and it was sad because I felt like it so didn't represent who I really was," Lopez said.[8]

Grossing a little more than $6 million, *Gigli* was considered a box office flop.

The professional break with Medina got ugly when Lopez accused him of not being licensed to act as her talent agent or manager. She claimed he collected fees for which he was not entitled, formally requesting the California labor commissioner to end any contracts for which Medina could still receive payment. Medina issued his own statement denying he had acted

> "I try not to take [media attention] too personally, because I don't think they do it just to me. But as a human being it feels like that. You feel like you're the only one being picked on. But the truth is, they pick on everybody. They really don't discriminate. I try to concentrate on all the great things I have going on in my life."[10]
>
> —JENNIFER LOPEZ

inappropriately, and he vowed to collect any money he was owed.

Another reason for the split was Lopez's interest in taking control of her career. But Lopez acknowledged Medina's role in her success, saying, "Benny is someone who has helped me, both personally and professionally, in countless ways, and I thank him profusely."[9]

Part of Lopez's new control included new business opportunities. In 2005, she expanded her brand by introducing a high-end fashion collection, called Sweetface, to her already blossoming fashion empire.

||||||||||||

Lopez displayed her dancing skills in *Shall We Dance*.

CHAPTER 7

Still Searching for Love

||||||||||||||||||||||||||||||||||||||||||||||

The very public end of her relationship with Affleck was hard on Lopez, but it taught her an important lesson about sharing too much personal information with the public. Lopez later said, "I learned you have to hold things closer to the cuff. There are things that are sacred and you have to keep them sacred for you."[1]

> "My life for me had become uncomfortable in the way it was affecting my personal life and the people in it, and so I decided I needed to take a look at that and my own responsibility in that. I realized there was a way to pull back from it in the way I lived."[3]
>
> —JENNIFER LOPEZ

As she had done after her previous breakups, Lopez threw herself back into work at the end of 2003. She began filming a new romantic comedy, *Shall We Dance,* costarring actors Richard Gere and Susan Sarandon. The film was an opportunity for Lopez to display her background as a dancer. Lopez also became reacquainted with someone she had not seen in five years, former boyfriend Marc Anthony. Anthony had been recruited to record a song with Lopez for the movie's sound track.

Immediately, Lopez and Anthony recognized the chemistry they had shared so many years ago was still there. As Anthony said, they had "matured enough" to finally be together.[2] They had similar values and upbringings, giving them many things in common. Lopez poured all her energy into the new romance.

MARC ANTHONY

Anthony is a singer, songwriter, producer, and actor. He is the top-selling salsa artist of all time. He was born Marco Antonio Muñiz in New York City on September 16, 1968, and is of Puerto Rican descent.

Anthony has earned five Grammy Awards and sold more than 11 million albums worldwide as of July 2012. In April 2012, Anthony received the Hall of Fame award at the *Billboard* Latin Music Awards.

Like her previous relationships, Lopez's romance with Anthony progressed quickly. In February 2004, Anthony proposed, and the couple married in a ceremony at their home on June 5, 2004, a surprise to most of their guests. They had not even publicly announced their engagement.

Following their marriage, the couple stayed out of the public eye for a while, but both continued to work. Creatively, Lopez's relationship with Anthony inspired a host of new projects, including her fourth album, *Rebirth*, which debuted at Number 2 on the *Billboard* chart on March 1, 2005. Lopez also premiered another film in May, the romantic comedy *Monster-in-Law*.

Lopez and Anthony reconnected in 2003, both personally and professionally.

BREAKING NEW GROUND

In 2005, Anthony and Lopez started collaborating on projects. They both starred in the biopic *El Cantante*, which was about 1970s salsa superstar Héctor Lavoe. It was also the first time Lopez served as a producer on a film, meaning she had the responsibility of hiring a director. She ultimately selected Leon Ichaso to direct the film. The love story between Lavoe and his girlfriend and eventual wife, Nilda "Puchi" Roman, was volatile. But that intensity was easy for real-life couple Anthony and Lopez to play because their chemistry was evident on screen.

Roman had been interviewed for the film shortly before her death in 2002. Lopez used the interview as research for her role, listening to the recordings over the course of several weeks to help put as much detail into her role as possible. *El Cantante* was released in 2006, and the film's sound track debuted at Number 1 on the *Billboard* Latin chart.

HÉCTOR LAVOE

Salsa superstar Héctor Lavoe was born on September 30, 1946, in Ponce, Puerto Rico. In 1963, he moved to New York City and discovered the Latin music scene. He had a talent for improvisation and joined salsa bandleader Willie Colón. Lavoe also discovered the drug scene and developed a heroin addiction. Lavoe had two children with two women in 1968—Carmen Ramírez and Nilda "Puchi" Roman. He had son Héctor Jr. with Roman and eventually married her, but kept a close relationship with Ramírez and their son, Juan Pérez. Colón dissolved the band because of Lavoe's drug use. Lavoe went solo, and in 1976, he could still sell out the largest soccer stadiums in Latin America. Audiences loved Lavoe, but his personal life grew more unstable and tragic. In 1988, Héctor Jr. died in an accident, and due to years of intravenous drug use, Lavoe contracted acquired immunodeficiency syndrome (AIDS). Lavoe died from complications of AIDS in 1993.

On April 11, 2007, Lopez appeared as a special guest on a Latin-music-themed episode of the television singing competition *American Idol*. She performed her single "Qué Hiciste" live, making her the first artist to sing a song on the show entirely in Spanish.

Anthony had also inspired Lopez to break new ground in her music career. He produced her first Spanish-language album, *Como Ama una Mujer*, which means, "How a Woman Loves." The album was released in March 2007, and debuted on the *Billboard* Latin chart at Number 1 during its opening week.

Como Ama una Mujer, however, did not perform as well commercially as Lopez's previous albums. On the *Billboard* Pop chart, the album debuted at Number 10, selling 48,000 copies its first week. That was significantly less than 2001's *J.Lo*, which debuted at Number 1 and sold more than 272,000 copies. However, Lopez joined a short list of only five artists to ever land in *Billboard*'s top ten with Spanish-language albums. The other four were rock band Maná and singers Shakira, Don Omar, and Selena.

On *El Cantante*, Lopez became a producer for the first time.

Lopez enjoyed recording the Spanish-language album—for her, it had been a long-time dream. With Anthony as her producer and cheerleader, Lopez was finally able to put her lingering doubts about singing behind her. "I think she really got to know her inner voice during that project," Anthony said of Lopez's newfound confidence. "Jennifer was always a singer, she was born a singer. Confidence is everything."[4]

|||||||||

Lopez embarked on her first tour in 2007, performing alongside Anthony.

CHAPTER 8

A Break from the Spotlight

||||||||||||||||||||||||||||||||||||||||||||||||||||||||||||||||||||||||||||||||||||

By 2007, Lopez's career had skyrocketed. Her music career had exceeded everyone's expectations, and she finally had a stable relationship with Anthony. She had a successful acting career and had become a fashion designer and perfumer. In 2007, *People en Español* listed her as the most influential person of Hispanic descent, honoring her for her contribution to the Hispanic community. Lopez was also ranked Number 9 on *Forbes'* list of the 20 Richest Women in Entertainment in 2007.

On October 9, 2007, Lopez released her sixth album, *Brave*. Debuting at Number 12 on the *Billboard* chart, it sold a disappointing 52,600 copies its first week. Critics criticized Lopez for her lack of lyrical depth, and unfortunately, fans agreed. *Brave* was her least commercially successful album.

HISPANIC PRIDE

On June 11, 2006, Lopez and Anthony surprised fans by serving as grand marshals, or honorary leaders, of New York City's National Puerto Rican Day Parade. Dozens of floats, dance troupes, and horses made their way along the parade route to the sounds of salsa music. Since then, they appeared in the 2007 and 2010 parades.

"I've never tried to hide the fact that I'm Latina," Lopez told *People en Español* in 2006. "I think that's why Hispanics are like, 'She's ours; she's out there, but she belongs to us'—and that's true. With the Latino community, I am theirs. I do belong to them—that's who I am."[1]

FIRST TOUR

After three years of marriage, Lopez and Anthony considered starting a family, but with a busy career, Lopez worried a family might be too much to hope for. But a conversation with her father changed her mind. David said simply, "Why can't you do both?"[2] It caused Lopez to consider why she thought it was impossible to have both a career and a family.

Because of her negative experiences with the tabloids, Lopez understood she needed to remain private about her personal life. Lopez said of being the center of media attention:

> It's a Pandora's box. It's a destructive lifestyle to be out there. I know because I've lived it. Being on the cover of the tabloids every day for two years—it's hard. You start forgetting who you really are inside.[3]

Eventually, Lopez became pregnant. Even as rumors swirled, Lopez and Anthony chose to keep the news of her pregnancy secret.

On September 28, 2007, Lopez and Anthony embarked on their El Cantante Tour together,

Lopez and Anthony kept news of her pregnancy quiet at first.

performing 20 shows throughout the United States and Canada. Not only was it their first tour together, it was also Lopez's first tour ever. At the tour's final concert in Miami on November 8, 2007, the couple decided they could not hide Lopez's expanding figure any longer. Lopez announced from the stage: "Marc and I are expecting a baby!"[4]

Once the tour ended, Lopez was ready for a break, later saying, "Once I did the tour, I really just wanted to shut it down . . . I was ready just to sit."[5] Her life was about to change.

|||||||||||||||||||||||||||||||||||||||||||||||||||||||||||

MOTHERHOOD

On February 22, 2008, Lopez gave birth to twins, son Maximilian David and daughter Emme Maribel. Lopez decided to take time away from work and the public eye to raise her children and do "nothing. I was like a wife and a mom," she said.[6]

After the birth of the twins, Lopez was not sure how long she wanted to stay home: "But you need

> "Children do something to you where you want to do everything right for them. And obviously no parent does everything right. It's this weird thing that happens where you are striving to be as good as you can be so they turn out well. And that requires that you be a really great, evolved, aware person in every moment. Which is pretty awesome. But it's also putting tremendous pressure on yourself—which is why women feel so guilty!"[7]
>
> —JENNIFER LOPEZ

that time to grow. You can't be afraid of, Oh, I'm out of the public, then I'm going to have to make a comeback. It's ridiculous. No."[8] Lopez was positive she would know when she was ready to go back to work.

Lopez had also reconciled with former manager and friend Medina when she was seven months pregnant. Lopez and Anthony named Medina godfather to their twins. "I just think of him as a real, creative soul mate. He's been the most consistent man in my life besides my dad," Lopez said of Medina.[9]

Following the birth of her twins, Lopez could not believe she ever had doubts about having both a career and a family. "I've always been the type that thinks you can have everything," she said. "There was never a doubt in my mind that you can

"We love each other. People always ask about all the men I dated, and I am like, 'You know the Benny and Jennifer story? That's the real story here.'"[10]

—JENNIFER LOPEZ

In September 2008, Lopez competed in the Nautica Malibu Triathlon, her first triathlon. She finished the half-mile (0.8 km) swim, 18-mile (29 km) bike ride, and 4-mile (6 km) run in 2 hours, 23 minutes, and 28 seconds. Lopez competed to raise money for Children's Hospital Los Angeles.

have an amazing career and an amazing family and have an amazing relationship."[11]

One of the effects of becoming a mother was the opportunity for Lopez to reconnect with her own mother—with whom she had always had a complicated relationship. Motherhood gave Lopez an appreciation of how Lupe felt about her and her sisters growing up. Lupe wrote to Lopez, "The way you feel about Max and Emme, I feel about you."[12] Lopez had never thought about it that way, and it touched her. She finally had an understanding of why her mother was sometimes so hard on her growing up.

||||||||||

Lopez hosted a release party for her 2011 album, *Love?*

CHAPTER 9

Staging a Comeback

||||||||||||||||||||||||||||||||||||||||||||||||||||||||||

n 2010, two years after the birth of the twins, Lopez was finally ready to return to work. But it wouldn't be easy. Lopez had been at the top of the entertainment world when she chose to take two years away from red carpets and the media spotlight. At age 40, many considered Lopez past her prime and weren't sure she would be able to climb her way back to the top.

In February 2010, Lopez decided to break away from Sony's Epic Records, her record company of 11 years and where she launched her singing career. Now, as she strategized her comeback, Lopez hoped for a fresh start by signing with Island Def Jam Records. Medina, who had been reinstated as Lopez's manager in 2008, was also instrumental in her move to the new record label, as well as numerous other deals.

> "I am conscious of the way I look when I go out. My mom and my grandma taught me that you never leave the house without taking a bath and at least attempting to fix your hair. I don't look like a glamour puss every day, but I try to look decent when I leave the house."[1]
>
> —JENNIFER LOPEZ

To Lopez, working on *Love?*, her seventh album overall and her first studio album in four years, felt like putting out her first record again. Her children and family inspired most of the songs on the album, which was ultimately released in April 2011. The songs on the album, Lopez said, "are all about love and the different things about it that can be confusing. The things that everyone wonders about. Is there a real true love? A once-in-a-lifetime thing?"[2]

She named one of the album's singles "Papi," explaining: "I always use the word *papi*; I call everyone 'papi.' I used to call Marc 'papi.' It was 'papi, papi, papi,' all the time."[3] She described the song as a celebration of loving someone.

The comeback strategy had a few false starts, however. Two advance singles, "Fresh Out of the Oven," and "Louboutins," performed disappointingly on the charts. However, "On the Floor," a single featuring rapper Pitbull, reminded fans and critics of Lopez's earlier dance beats such as "Waiting for Tonight" from 1999. "On the Floor" was her tenth single to reach the top ten on *Billboard*.

"ON THE FLOOR"

In March 2011, Lopez's first top ten single in eight years, "On the Floor," entered the *Billboard* singles charts at Number 9. It sold more than 3 million copies in the United States. The video for "On the Floor" had more than 500 million hits on YouTube as of July 2012—the second most popular clip on YouTube ever.

The Back-up Plan was Lopez's first film in four years.

The Back-up Plan, a romantic comedy released on April 23, 2010, was Lopez's first film after having the twins. *The Back-Up Plan* generally received poor reviews, but it debuted in second place at the box office and earned more than $77 million worldwide. Lopez played Zoe, a single woman in her thirties who decides to have a child on her own. Lopez drew on her own pregnancy for inspiration for the character, saying: "I had so much experience to bring to the role."[4]

ENDORSEMENTS AND PHILANTHROPY

When Lopez announced her return to the public eye, Medina started lining up endorsement deals. Celebrities such as Lopez often endorse products, which can mean big sales to a company. In 2010, with the help of Medina's behind-the-scenes negotiations, Lopez landed deals with women's razor Gillette Venus, fashion company Gucci, and cosmetics company L'Oréal. Medina commented on Lopez's strength of commitment, saying, "And she never half does anything. When she commits to

VENUS AMBASSADOR

In February 2011, Gillette, manufacturer of Venus razors for women, introduced Lopez as the first-ever global ambassador for its Venus Goddess Fund for Education. As global ambassador, Lopez helped spread knowledge about educational opportunities for women. The core mission of the Venus program is to provide a "strong foundation for future success, and each of these organizations teaches and empowers women to excel in unique ways, whether via mentorship, schooling or even healthcare for their children."[8]

anything in her work, her life, or her relationships, she is in it."[5]

Inspired by motherhood, Lopez created the Lopez Family Foundation with her sister Lynda in June 2010. Lynda also had a daughter, Lucie, in September 2008. The organization is dedicated to "improving the health and well-being of women and children including raising the level of medical care available to them."[6] Lopez said, "We both feel the desire, as never before, to help create a healthier, happier environment for others."[7]

Over the years, Lopez has supported several charities, including Amnesty International and

Children's Health Fund's Operation Assist following the devastation of Hurricane Katrina in 2005. Lopez has also generously donated money to the March of Dimes, American Red Cross, City of Hope, Love Our Children USA, and United Nations Children's Fund (UNICEF), among others.

Lopez's comeback was almost complete. Next would come a foray into reality television. Little did she know it would help make her the "world's greatest musical comeback act."[9]

||||||||||

FOX

Lopez was announced as
a new *American Idol* judge
in September 2010.

CHAPTER 10

American Idol and Beyond

||||||||||||||||||||||||||||||||||||||||||||||||||||||||||||||||||

n June 2010, Medina arranged for Lopez to meet with producers from the hit television singing competition *American Idol*. When three of the show's four judges who appeared during its ninth season announced their departures in 2010, producers began searching for new judges to take their places.

Lopez was not a stranger to the reality show. In 2007, she had appeared on

American Idol as a mentor to the top eight finalists during season six's Latin Week. She surprised viewers and contestants with her warm, candid personality. Lopez had helped the contestants through a challenging genre of music by offering the advice that "key to any type of Latin themed music is the passion."[1]

AMERICAN IDOL JUDGE

Lopez was officially announced as a new judge on *American Idol* in September 2010. After signing a

AMERICAN IDOL

British music producer Simon Fuller developed *American Idol* as an American version of his popular British television show, *Pop Idol*. Along with friend and music partner Simon Cowell, Fuller pitched the show to American television producers. It took several rounds of pitching before he received any interest, but the show finally debuted on the Fox network in 2002.

Fuller created the concept of group auditions, judging, and audience voting. Adding the participants' backstories to create a real-life soap opera effect helped complete the package. Famous contestants of *American Idol* include Kelly Clarkson, Carrie Underwood, Chris Daughtry, Ruben Studdard, Jordin Sparks, Kellie Pickler, and Jennifer Hudson.

$12 million deal with the show, Lopez admitted, "I never thought about being a judge on *American Idol*. I was a mentor, and I enjoyed doing that. . . . But I'd never thought about being a judge, so this was all a big surprise for me."[2]

In January 2011, *American Idol* kicked off its tenth season with two newcomers joining original *Idol* judge Randy Jackson and host Ryan Seacrest: Lopez and Steven Tyler from the rock band Aerosmith. The world was about to see Lopez in a different way. Nigel Lythgoe, an executive producer for *American Idol*, praised Lopez as she began her judging role, saying, "She's listening to what they say and how they sound and commenting and being Jennifer Lopez. She's seen the program and she knows what she's doing and she is taking it seriously."[3]

"[Lopez] comes off as very strong, with a lot of conviction, and very believable. Hence, the American public has fallen in love with her."[4]

—AMERICAN IDOL *JUDGE STEVEN TYLER*

Lopez enjoyed working with her fellow *Idol* judges, Tyler, *left,* and Jackson, *right.*

When original *Idol* judge Simon Cowell, who was considered the most critical judge, left after nine seasons, the media speculated about the show's ratings with the new judges. Some speculated that Cowell's criticism kept the show interesting. However, Lopez and Tyler helped the show continue as the highest-rated show amongst its competition, and the ratings increased by 4 percent after their debut as judges. Perhaps the audience was ready for a friendlier *Idol*—or perhaps having a harsher judge on the show had simply run its course.

Joining the show could have been a career killer, but the risk paid off for Lopez. Lopez said of being a judge, "I'm really loving finding and being touched by great talent when it walks in the room. It's really exciting to be a part of that."[5]

¡Q'VIVA! THE CHOSEN

In June 2011, Lopez and Anthony announced they were launching a new project together, *¡Q'Viva! The Chosen*. The reality show would be a 21-country search to celebrate Latin music, artistry, and dance. *¡Q'Viva!* also introduced a unique interactive component, by encouraging entertainers to submit auditions via YouTube and allowing public nominations on the social networking site Facebook. The show followed Anthony and Lopez during the summer of 2011 as they traveled extensively around Latin American countries searching for talent.

Unfortunately, Lopez and Anthony announced their marriage was ending in July 2011. But Lopez said she would always respect Anthony and maintain a close relationship with him. "He will always be in our lives," Lopez said. "He will always hold a special place in my heart as the father of my children."[6] In fact, Lopez and Anthony continued working together on *¡Q'Viva!*, and Lopez has said they remain friends.

During Lopez's time as a judge on *American Idol*, the public was able to catch a glimpse of the real woman behind the fame. To the surprise of some critics, Lopez's observations and critiques about contestants came across as real and sincere. Lopez was surprised as well that people did not know her, saying, "So this is a great time because I feel like people really, finally know me."[7]

GLOWING

In May 2012, Lopez introduced the eighteenth fragrance, Glowing, to her perfume line. Lopez's fragrance line generates more than $100 million in sales for Coty each year. Lopez receives approximately $5 million annually from her fragrance line.

MOST BEAUTIFUL PERSON

People magazine placed Lopez at the very top of its annual Most Beautiful list in 2011. In her interview with the magazine, Lopez emphasized she works hard to stay fit, saying, "I don't want anybody thinking it's easy. It does take time and it's hard work. . . . "[8]

Lopez also released her seventeenth fragrance, Love and Light, on the Home Shopping Network (HSN) in July 2011. It had been almost ten years since the launch of Lopez's first fragrance, Glow.

In 2011, Lopez signed on to judge a second season of *American Idol*, earning $20 million. With her numerous endorsement deals, movies, records, and *American Idol*, Lopez earned $52 million in 2011. She also launched a clothing line specifically for Kohl's department stores.

All of Lopez's hard work paid off in 2012, when *Forbes* magazine ranked Lopez number one on its annual "Celebrity 100," a list of the most powerful and influential celebrities in the world. Lopez also added two more movies to her acting résumé in 2012: *What to Expect When You're Expecting* and the animated *Ice Age: Continental Drift*.

Lopez performed in Toronto during her first international tour, Dance Again World Tour.

THE FUTURE

On July 13, 2012, Lopez officially announced she would not be returning to *American Idol* for its twelfth season. Tyler had also decided to step down as judge on the show. Of her decision to leave the show, Lopez said, "The time has come for me to get back to the other things that I do. . . . We had an amazing run."[9] But Lopez was also grateful to the show, which had helped reinvigorate her career.

Lopez had already changed things up. She launched her first international tour, Dance Again World Tour, which opened in Panama City, Panama, on June 14, 2012. As for the future, Lopez

> "You're in competition with nobody but yourself. Something that's for you is for you, and nobody can take it away from you. You just have to believe in that, you have to believe in that destiny. And something that wasn't for you, that somebody else gets, you just have to know it was never meant for you."[12]
>
> —*JENNIFER LOPEZ*

had said she hoped to have time to star in more films. "I do miss doing films," she said. "I feel like the last two years with *American Idol*, I've really, really focused on, you know, my music."[10]

Lopez has been a singer, actress, philanthropist, producer, and more in her career. She is also a mother, a sister, and a daughter. By working hard and persisting, Lopez hopes she can be a role model for women, saying,

> *I want to be remembered as a symbol that you can accomplish whatever you want and that you don't have to be just one thing. You don't have to be labeled. Life is there to be eaten up by you— it's your choice.*[11]

||||||||||

TIMELINE

1969

Jennifer Lynn
Lopez is born on
July 24 in the Bronx,
New York City.

1986

Lopez leaves
home to pursue
a career in acting
and dancing.

1991

Lopez becomes
a Fly Girl on *In
Living Color*.

1999

On the 6, Lopez's
first album, is
released June 1. Its
single "If You Had My
Love" hits Number 1
on the *Billboard*
chart on June 12.

1999

Lopez begins dating
Sean Combs and
hires manager
Benny Medina.

1999

Lopez is arrested
after a nightclub
incident while
with Combs on
December 27.

1997	**1997**	**1998**
Lopez marries Ojani Noa in February, but the marriage ends 11 months later.	*Selena* premiers in March.	Lopez receives a Golden Globe nomination for her performance in *Selena*.

2000	**2001**	**2001**
Lopez wears a revealing green chiffon Versace dress to the Grammy Awards on February 23.	Lopez simultaneously has the Number 1 album, *J.Lo*, and top movie, *The Wedding Planner*, when both debut in January.	Lopez marries dancer Cris Judd on September 29, but the marriage ends nine months later.

TIMELINE

2002

2002

2003

Lopez starts dating *Gigli* costar Ben Affleck.

Glow, Lopez's first fragrance, is released in September.

Lopez cancels her wedding to Affleck in September.

2008

2010

2011

Twins Max and Emme are born to Lopez and Anthony on February 22.

Lopez becomes a judge on season ten of *American Idol*.

Lopez's single "On the Floor" is released March 3, reaching Number 9 on the singles charts.

2004	**2007**	**2007**
Lopez marries Marc Anthony on June 5.	*People en Español* calls Lopez the most influential person of Hispanic descent.	In March, Lopez's first Spanish-language album, *Como Ama una Mujer*, debuts on the *Billboard* Latin Chart at Number 1.

2011	**2012**	**2012**
Lopez and Anthony announce their divorce in July.	*Forbes* lists Lopez at the top of their annual Celebrity 100 list.	Lopez announces her departure from *American Idol* and launches her first international tour in June.

GET THE SCOOP

FULL NAME

Jennifer Lynn Lopez

DATE OF BIRTH

July 24, 1969

PLACE OF BIRTH

Bronx, New York

SELECTED ALBUMS

On the 6 (1999), *J.Lo* (2001), *This Is Me . . . Then* (2002), *Rebirth* (2005), *Brave* (2007), *Love?* (2011)

SELECTED FILMS AND TELEVISION APPEARANCES

Selena (1997), *Out of Sight* (1998), *The Wedding Planner* (2001), *Enough* (2002), *Maid in Manhattan* (2002), *Shall We Dance* (2004), *Monster-in-Law* (2005), *The Back-up Plan* (2010), *American Idol* (2011–2012), *What to Expect When You're Expecting* (2012)

SELECTED AWARDS

- Won the 1999 *Billboard* Music Video Award for Best Pop Video Clip for "If You Had My Love"
- Won the 2000 MTV Video Music Award for Best Dance Video for "Waiting For Tonight"

- Nominated for 1998 Golden Globe for Best Performance by an Actress in a Motion Picture—Musical or Comedy for *Selena* (1997)
- Nominated for 2000 Grammy for Best Dance Recording for "Waiting for Tonight"

BUSINESS

Lopez launched her own clothing line, J.Lo by Jennifer Lopez, in 2001. It includes clothing, swimwear, and accessories. Lopez also debuted her first fragrance, Glow by J.Lo, in 2002. Lopez earns an estimated $5 million from her fragrance line, which introduced its eighteenth fragrance in May 2012.

PHILANTHROPY

Lopez supports the Children's Hospital Los Angeles and participated in the Nautica Malibu Triathlon benefitting the hospital in 2008. Lopez and her sister Lynda founded the Lopez Family Foundation in June 2010, to improve the health and well-being of women and children. In February 2011, she became the first Global Ambassador for Gillette's Venus Goddess Fund for Education, spreading knowledge about educational opportunities for women.

"You can't have big ups without big downs."

—JENNIFER LOPEZ

GLOSSARY

audition—A trial hearing given to a singer, actor, or other performer to test suitability for a role, professional training, or competition.

Billboard—A music chart system used by the music recording industry to measure record popularity or sales.

chart—A weekly listing of songs or albums in order of popularity or record sales.

debut—A first appearance.

genre—A category of art, music, or literature characterized by a particular style, form, or content.

hip-hop—A style of popular music associated with US urban culture that features rap spoken against a background of electronic music or beats.

mentor—A person with experience in a specific field, who guides someone with less experience.

monogamy—The practice of having a romantic relationship with only one person at a time.

paparazzi—Aggressive photojournalists who take pictures of celebrities and sell them to media outlets.

pop—A commercial or popular style of music.

producer—Someone who oversees or provides money for a play, television show, movie, or album.

record label—A brand or trademark related to the marketing of music videos and recordings.

salsa—Music of Latin American origin that combines influences from R&B, jazz, and rock music.

single—An individual song that is distributed on its own over the radio and other mediums.

ADDITIONAL RESOURCES

SELECTED BIBLIOGRAPHY

"Jennifer Lopez (Ep. 215)." *Behind The Music*. VH1, 8 July 2010. Web. 30 July 2012.

Karger, Dave. "Biopicked for Stardom." *Entertainment Weekly*. Entertainment Weekly, 9 Aug. 1996. Web. 24 Apr. 2012.

Van Meter, Jonathan. "Jennifer Lopez: Venus Rising." *Vogue*. Vogue, 15 Mar. 2012. Web. 20 May 2012.

FURTHER READINGS

Dougherty, Terri. *The 20th Century's Most Influential Hispanics: Jennifer Lopez, Entertainer*. Detroit: Lucent, 2008. Print.

Novas, Hilmice, and Rosemary Silva. *Remembering Selena*. New York: St. Martin's Griffin, 1995. Print.

WEB SITES

To learn more about Jennifer Lopez, visit ABDO Publishing Company online at **www.abdopublishing.com**. Web sites about Jennifer Lopez are featured on our Book Links page. These links are routinely monitored and updated to provide the most current information available.

PLACES TO VISIT

The Grammy Museum
800 West Olympic Boulevard, Los Angeles, CA 90015
213-765-6800
www.grammymuseum.org
Celebrates and explores the legacy of all music genres and
the history of the recording industry.

Madame Tussauds New York
234 West Forty-Second Street, New York, NY 10036
866-841-3505
www.madametussauds.com/NewYork
Lopez's wax statue is on display with other celebrity wax
figures at this famous wax museum.

SOURCE NOTES

CHAPTER 1. ON THE BRINK OF STARDOM

1. Henri Behar. "Jennifer Lopez on 'Selena.'" *Film Scouts Interviews*. Film Scouts Interviews, 1997. Web. 24 Apr. 2012.

2. Dave Karger. "Biopicked for Stardom." *Entertainment Weekly*. Entertainment Weekly, 9 Aug. 1996. Web. 24 Apr. 2012.

3. Ibid.

4. Pam Lambert and Betty Cortina. "Viva Selena!" *People* 47.11 (1997): 160. *MasterFILE Premier*. Web. 25 July 2012.

5. "Jennifer Lopez (Ep. 215)." *Behind The Music*. VH1, 8 July 2010. Web. 30 July 2012.

6. "*Selena*: About the Production." *Film Scouts*. Film Scouts LLC, n.d. Web. 11 May 2012.

7. Henri Behar. "Jennifer Lopez on 'Selena.'" *Film Scouts Interviews*. Film Scouts Interviews, 1997. Web. 24 Apr. 2012.

8. "Jennifer Lopez (Ep. 215)." *Behind The Music*. VH1, 8 July 2010. Web. 30 July 2012.

9. Roger Ebert. "Review of Selena." *Chicago Sun-Times*. Chicago Sun-Times, 21 Mar. 1997. Web. 21 May 2012.

10. "Jennifer Lopez (Ep. 215)." *Behind The Music*. VH1, 8 July 2010. Web. 30 July 2012.

CHAPTER 2. EARLY YEARS

1. "Jennifer Lopez (Ep. 215)." *Behind The Music*. VH1, 8 July 2010. Web. 30 July 2012.

2. Ibid.

3. Ibid.

4. Ibid.

5. Ibid.

6. Henri Behar. "Jennifer Lopez on 'Selena.'" *Film Scouts Interviews*. Film Scouts Interviews, 1997. Web. 24 Apr. 2012.

7. "*Selena*: About the Production." *Film Scouts*. Film Scouts LLC, n.d. Web. 11 May 2012.

CHAPTER 3. MAKING MUSIC

1. "Jennifer Lopez (Ep. 215)." *Behind The Music*. VH1, 8 July 2010. Web. 30 July 2012.

2. Ibid.

3. "*Anaconda*: About the Production." *Film Scouts*. Film Scouts LLC, n.d. Web. 11 May 2012.

4. Martha Frankel. "Jennifer Lopez Loves To." *Cosmopolitan* 226.3 (1999): 202. *MasterFILE Premier*. Web. 24 July 2012.

5. "Jennifer Lopez (Ep. 215)." *Behind The Music*. VH1, 8 July 2010. Web. 30 July 2012.

6. Ibid.

7. Elysa Gardner and Sante D'Orazio. "She's All That." *InStyle* 6.6 (1999): 276. *MasterFILE Premier*. Web. 24 July 2012.

8. "Jennifer Lopez (Ep. 215)." *Behind The Music*. VH1, 8 July 2010. Web. 30 July 2012.

CHAPTER 4. JUGGLING MUSIC AND MOVIES

1. "Donatella Versace." *Voguepedia*. Vogue, n.d. Web. 21 May 2012.

2. "Jennifer Lopez (Ep. 215)." *Behind The Music*. VH1, 8 July 2010. Web. 30 July 2012.

3. Ibid.

CHAPTER 5. *J.LO* ON TOP

1. "Jennifer Lopez (Ep. 215)." *Behind The Music*. VH1, 8 July 2010. Web. 30 July 2012.

2. Jim Ferguson. "StudioLA's Jim Ferguson Interviews Jennifer Lopez Star of *The Wedding Planner*." *AsianConnections*. StudioLA, n.d. Web. 20 May 2012.

3. "Jennifer Lopez (Ep. 215)." *Behind The Music*. VH1, 8 July 2010. Web. 30 July 2012.

4. Michelle Tauber. "J.Lo Goes it Alone." *People*. People, 24 June 2002. Web. 21 May 2012.

5. "Jennifer Lopez (Ep. 215)." *Behind The Music*. VH1, 8 July 2010. Web. 30 July 2012.

6. Peter Rubin. "Dream Catcher." *Elle*. Elle, 26 Sept. 2008. Web. 28 May 2012.

7. "Jennifer Lopez (Ep. 215)." *Behind The Music*. VH1, 8 July 2010. Web. 30 July 2012.

8. Ibid.

9. "Jennifer Lopez on New Movie 'Enough." *ABC News*. ABC News, 22 May 2002. Web. 30 July 2012.

10. "Jennifer Lopez Lyrics: 'Jenny From The Block.'"*AZLyrics.com*. AZLyrics.com, n.d. Web. 27 Jul 2012.

CHAPTER 6. BUILDING A BRAND

1. "Jennifer Lopez (Ep. 215)." *Behind The Music*. VH1, 8 July 2010. Web. 30 July 2012.

2. Ibid.

3. Ibid.

4. Ibid.

5. Ibid.

6. "Blame Bennifer: Celeb Uni-Names Multiply." *Fox News*. Fox News, 13 June 2005. Web. 30 July 2012.

7. "Jennifer Lopez (Ep. 215)." *Behind The Music*. VH1, 8 July 2010. Web. 30 July 2012.

8. Jonathan Van Meter. "Jennifer Lopez: Venus Rising." *Vogue*. Vogue, 15 Mar. 2012. Web. 20 May 2012.

9. Leo Ebersole and Kris Karnopp. "Guess We Can Start Calling Her Jenny from the . . ." *Chicago Tribune*. Chicago Tribune, 12 June 2003. Web. 30 July 2012.

10. Julie Naughton and Pete Born. "Getting to the Heart of J.Lo." *Women's Wear Daily*. Condé Nast, 9 Feb. 2012. Web. 30 July 2012.

CHAPTER 7. STILL SEARCHING FOR LOVE

1. "Jennifer Lopez (Ep. 215)." *Behind The Music*. VH1, 8 July 2010. Web. 30 July 2012.

2. Ibid.

3. Rob Owen. "Tuned In: Lopez Back in Spotlight with MTV's 'DanceLife.'" *Pittsburgh Post-Gazette*. Pittsburgh Post-Gazette, 13 Jan. 2007. Web. 30 July 2012.

4. "Jennifer Lopez (Ep. 215)." *Behind The Music*. VH1, 8 July 2010. Web. 30 July 2012.

CHAPTER 8. A BREAK FROM THE SPOTLIGHT

1. Richard Pérez-Feria. "Jennifer Lopez: The Interview." *People En Español*. People, 25 Apr. 2006. Web. 30 July 2012.

2. Lori Berger. "'What To Expect' Stars Aren't Afraid of the Unexpected." *Redbook*. Redbook, n.d. Web. 30 July 2012.

3. Stephen Silverman. "Jennifer Lopez: Who Didn't Know I Was Pregnant." *People*. People, 9 Jan. 2008. Web. 23 May 2012.

4. Ibid.

5. Ibid.

6. Candice Rainey. "Jennifer Lopez." *Elle*. Elle, 5 Jan. 2010. Web. 30 July 2012.

7. Jonathan Van Meter. "Jennifer Lopez: Venus Rising." *Vogue*. Vogue, 15 Mar. 2012. Web. 20 May 2012.

8. Candice Rainey. "Jennifer Lopez." *Elle*. Elle, 5 Jan. 2010. Web. 30 July 2012.

9. Jonathan Van Meter. "Jennifer Lopez: Venus Rising." *Vogue*. Vogue, 15 Mar. 2012. Web. 20 May 2012.

10. Ibid.

11. "Jennifer Lopez (Ep. 215)." *Behind The Music*. VH1, 8 July 2010. Web. 30 July 2012.

12. Ibid.

CHAPTER 9. STAGING A COMEBACK

1. Lesley Goober. "Jennifer Gets It Right." *Cosmopolitan*. Hearst Communications, n.d. Web. 30 July 2012.

2. John Dingwall. "Jennifer Lopez: I Love Being a Mum . . . But I'm Happy Being a Singer Again." *DailyRecord.co.uk*. Daily Record, 15 Mar. 2010. Web. 30 July 2012.

3. "Jennifer Lopez Explains Marc Anthony-Inspired New Song 'Papi.'" *Access Hollywood*. NBC Universal, 2 Sept. 2011. Web. 30 July 2012.

4. Cindy Clark. "First Look: Jennifer Lopez Starring in 'The Back-Up Plan.'" *USA Today*. Gannett, 12 Feb. 2010. Web. 30 July 2012.

5. Jonathan Van Meter. "Jennifer Lopez: Venus Rising." *Vogue*. Vogue, 15 Mar. 2012. Web. 20 May 2012.

6. "Gillette Venus Announces Jennifer Lopez as First-Ever Global Ambassador." *P&G Corporate Newsroom*. P&G, 3 Feb. 2011. Web. 30 July 2012.

7. Jennifer Lopez. "A Letter from Jennifer." *Lopez Family Foundation*. Lopez Family Foundation, n.d. Web. 30 May 2012.

8. "Gillette Venus Announces Jennifer Lopez as First-Ever Global Ambassador." *P&G Corporate Newsroom*. P&G, 3 Feb. 2011. Web. 30 July 2012.

9. Gerrick D. Kennedy. "Jennifer Lopez Named 'World's Greatest Musical Comeback Act'—Seriously." *Los Angeles Times*. Los Angeles Times, 13 Dec. 2011. Web. 30 July 2012.

CHAPTER 10. *AMERICAN IDOL* AND BEYOND

1. "Jennifer Lopez Coaching on *American Idol* (April 10) 2007." *YouTube*. YouTube, 11 Apr. 2007. Web. 30 July 2012.

2. "Jennifer Lopez–American Idol Promo Interview." *YouTube*. YouTube, 21 Jan. 2011. Web. 30 July 2012.

3. Lynette Rice. "Nigel Lythgoe on New 'American Idol' Judges: No Softies on the Panel!" *Entertainment Weekly*. Entertainment Weekly, 10 Nov. 2010. Web. 30 July 2012.

4. Jonathan Van Meter. "Jennifer Lopez: Venus Rising." *Vogue*. Vogue, 15 Mar. 2012. Web. 20 May 2012.

5. "Jennifer Lopez–American Idol Promo Interview." *YouTube*. YouTube, 21 Jan. 2011. Web. 30 July 2012.

6. "Jennifer Lopez Give Vanity Fair Her First Interview Since Announcing Her Divorce from Marc Anthony." *Vanity Fair*. Vanity Fair, 2 Aug. 2011. Web. 2 June 2012.

7. Jonathan Van Meter. "Jennifer Lopez: Venus Rising." *Vogue*. Vogue, 15 Mar. 2012. Web. 20 May 2012.

8. Julie Jordan. "Jennifer Lopez: Being Beautiful is 'Part of my Job'." *People*. People, 13 Apr. 2011. Web. 2 June 2012.

9. Erin Strecker. "Jennifer Lopez Leaving 'American Idol': 'The Time Has Come.'" *Entertainment Weekly*. Entertainment Weekly, 13 July 2012. Web. 30 July 2012.

10. Nekesa Mumbi Moody. "With 'American Idol' Behind Her, Jennifer Lopez Eyes More Films." *Entertainment Weekly*. Entertainment Weekly, 16 July 2012. Web. 30 July 2012.

11. Lori Berger. "Jennifer Lopez: Why She's Not Giving Up the Spotlight for the Sandbox." *Redbook*. Redbook, n.d. Web. 30 July 2012.

12. "Jennifer Lopez–American Idol Promo Interview." *YouTube*. YouTube, 21 Jan. 2011. Web. 30 July 2012.

INDEX

ABOUT THE AUTHOR

Kristine Carlson Asselin is the author of a dozen children's books for the school library and elementary markets. In addition to nonfiction, she also writes young adult and middle grade fiction, as well as the occasional picture book. She has a BS from Fitchburg State University and an MA from the University of Connecticut.

PHOTO CREDITS